THIS JOUR

_____

AND

_____

We can use this journal to write to each other.
You can write about anything you want, anytime you want.
When you want me to read it, put it in our special place. When I write back, I'll put it back for you.
We can keep it somewhere safe when we aren't writing so nobody else can read it!

RULES

Who is allowed to see this book?

How will you pass the journal back and forth?

When can you expect a response?

Where are we going to keep the journal safe when we are not using it?

What are you going to use to write with?

MOM

DATE

MOM

DATE

ME

DATE

MOM

DATE

MOM

DATE

MOM

DATE

MOM

DATE

MOM

DATE

MOM

DATE

MOM

DATE

MOM

DATE

MOM

DATE

MOM

DATE

MOM

DATE

MOM

DATE

MOM

DATE

MOM

DATE

MOM

DATE

MOM

DATE

MOM

DATE

ME

DATE

MOM

DATE

MOM

DATE

MOM

DATE

MOM

DATE

ME

DATE

MOM

DATE

MOM

DATE

I MISS YOU DURING THE DAY BECAUSE...

ME: **DATE**

MOM: **DATE**

WHAT DOES BEING A GOOD FRIEND LOOK LIKE?

ME: **DATE**

MOM: **DATE**

WHAT ARE 5 THINGS YOU ARE GRATEFUL FOR?

ME: **DATE**

_____

_____

_____

_____

_____

_____

MOM: **DATE**

_____

_____

_____

_____

_____

_____

MY FAVORITE SUBJECT IS / WAS...

ME: **DATE**

MOM: **DATE**

WHAT IS ONE ACTIVITY YOU WANT TO DO AS A FAMILY?

ME: **DATE**

MOM: **DATE**

DESCRIBE YOUR FAVORITE WAY TO SPEND A COLD, RAINY DAY?

ME: **DATE**

MOM: **DATE**

WHAT SCARES YOU THE MOST?

ME: **DATE**

_____

_____

_____

_____

_____

_____

_____

MOM: **DATE**

_____

_____

_____

_____

_____

_____

WHAT MAKES YOU FEEL LOVED?

ME: DATE

_____
_____
_____
_____
_____
_____
_____

MOM: DATE

_____
_____
_____
_____
_____
_____

I'M PROUD OF YOU BECAUSE...

ME: **DATE**

_____
_____
_____
_____
_____
_____
_____

MOM: **DATE**

_____
_____
_____
_____
_____
_____
_____

WHAT DO YOU LIKE THE MOST ABOUT YOURSELF?

ME: **DATE**

MOM: **DATE**

WHAT KIND OF MUSIC DO YOU LIKE THE BEST?

ME: **DATE**

MOM: **DATE**

IF YOU COULD TAKE A TRIP ANYWHERE, WHERE WOULD YOU GO?

ME:　　　　　　　　　　**DATE**

MOM:　　　　　　　　　**DATE**

WHO DO YOU FIND INSPIRATIONAL?

ME: **DATE**

MOM: **DATE**

WHAT WOULD YOU CHANGE ABOUT YOURSELF IF YOU COULD?

ME: DATE

MOM: DATE

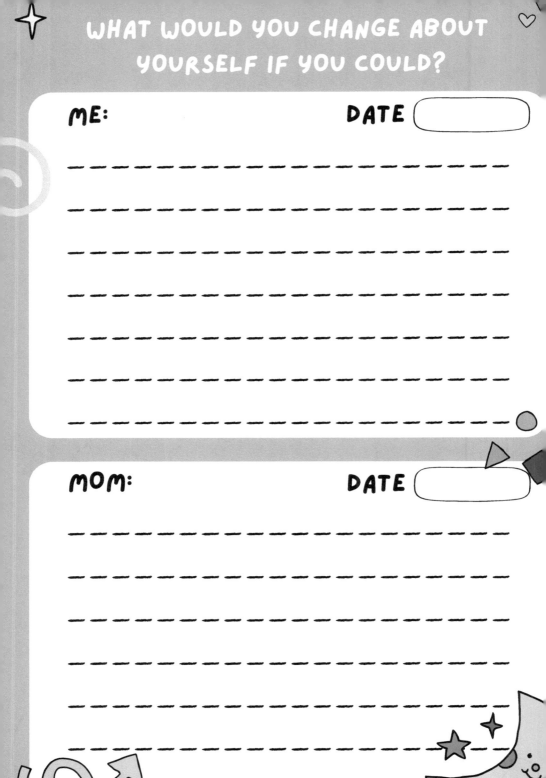

A QUESTION FROM ME TO YOU

QUESTION:

FROM......................... TO...............................

_____

_____

_____

_____

_____

_____

ANSWER:

_____

_____

_____

_____

_____

_____

A QUESTION FROM ME TO YOU

QUESTION:

FROM........................ TO................................

ANSWER:

A QUESTION FROM ME TO YOU

QUESTION:

FROM........................ TO...............................

_____

_____

_____

_____

_____

_____

ANSWER:

_____

_____

_____

_____

_____

_____

A QUESTION FROM ME TO YOU

QUESTION:

FROM........................ TO................................

ANSWER:

A QUESTION FROM ME TO YOU

QUESTION:

FROM........................ TO................................

_____

_____

_____

_____

_____

_____

ANSWER:

_____

_____

_____

_____

_____

_____

A QUESTION FROM ME TO YOU

QUESTION:

FROM.......................   TO................................

_____

_____

_____

_____

_____

_____

ANSWER:

_____

_____

_____

_____

_____

_____

A QUESTION FROM ME TO YOU

QUESTION:

FROM........................ TO................................

ANSWER:

A QUESTION FROM ME TO YOU

QUESTION:

FROM........................ TO................................

ANSWER:

A QUESTION FROM ME TO YOU

QUESTION:

FROM......................... TO...............................

_____

_____

_____

_____

_____

_____

ANSWER:

_____

_____

_____

_____

_____

_____

A QUESTION FROM ME TO YOU

QUESTION:

FROM........................ TO................................

_____

_____

_____

_____

_____

_____

ANSWER:

_____

_____

_____

_____

_____

_____

A QUESTION FROM ME TO YOU

QUESTION:

FROM........................ TO................................

ANSWER:

A QUESTION FROM ME TO YOU

QUESTION:

FROM........................ TO...............................

_____

_____

_____

_____

_____

_____

ANSWER:

_____

_____

_____

_____

_____

_____

A QUESTION FROM ME TO YOU

QUESTION:

FROM........................ TO..............................

ANSWER:

A QUESTION FROM ME TO YOU

QUESTION:

FROM........................ TO..............................

_____

_____

_____

_____

_____

_____

ANSWER:

_____

_____

_____

_____

_____

_____

A QUESTION FROM ME TO YOU

QUESTION:

FROM........................ TO................................

_____

_____

_____

_____

_____

_____

ANSWER:

_____

_____

_____

_____

_____

_____

A QUESTION FROM ME TO YOU

QUESTION:

FROM...................... TO..............................

_____

_____

_____

_____

_____

ANSWER:

_____

_____

_____

_____

_____

_____

A QUESTION FROM ME TO YOU

QUESTION:

FROM........................ TO................................

_____

_____

_____

_____

_____

_____

ANSWER:

_____

_____

_____

_____

_____

_____

A QUESTION FROM ME TO YOU

QUESTION:

FROM........................ TO................................

ANSWER:

A QUESTION FROM ME TO YOU

QUESTION:

FROM........................ TO................................

ANSWER:

A QUESTION FROM ME TO YOU

QUESTION:

FROM........................ TO................................

_____

_____

_____

_____

_____

_____

ANSWER:

_____

_____

_____

_____

_____

_____

A QUESTION FROM ME TO YOU

QUESTION:

FROM........................ TO..............................

ANSWER:

Made in United States
Troutdale, OR
07/15/2023

11295369R00066